Gathering Island Way

By Patricia M Gabey (Nay-Ama)
Illustrated by Tanya Zeinalova

We respect and honour Aboriginal and Torres Strait Islander Elders past, present and future. We acknowledge the stories, traditions and living cultures of Aboriginal and Torres Strait Islander peoples on this land and commit to building a brighter future together.

Library For All Ltd.

I was so excited, today was the day!

I could feel my heart beat quickly as I woke up and sprang out of bed.

I was finally old enough to go and visit my aunty to learn traditional ways of hunting and gathering food. I call my aunty 'Aka'.

I had been waiting for this for the past year.

All of the women in our family learn our traditional gathering ways from each other. Our aunties, grandmas and mothers are our teachers.

I put my island dress on and ran through the kitchen. I grabbed a banana for breakfast, kissing my mum goodbye, as I dashed through the front door. Off I went, down the street to Aka's house.

I got through the gates, yelling, "I'm here, Aka! I'm here!"

Aka greeted me at the door with a kiss and a hug.

"OK, my girl," Aka said. "Let's go! Today, I'll show you how to find cashew nuts and *katai*."

"What is *katai*?" I asked.

"Yams, my girl," said Aka. "Now, follow me out to the garden."

We walked through Aka's overgrown garden.

Already, there was plenty to see and eat.

"Be careful where you walk," Aka advised. "Follow my every step, so the wrong plants don't touch your legs and hurt you." Then, she crouched down. "Look, look, here is the yam vine!"

"Be careful to follow the vine to the ground," said Aka, following the vine with her finger in the air. "The vine has thorns, so you must be careful to find them and pick them off. We don't want you getting hurt."

I found another vine and followed it to the ground, snapping off the tiny thorns with a small knife.

I smiled with delight as Aka came over to help me pull the root of the vine from the ground.

"One, two, three, pull!"

We both fell to the ground with laughter.

The yam's root was stuck.

We gave it another pull...

And it was set free from the dirt.

Aka said, "It's important we wash the *katai* thoroughly before we can cook it, to remove the slime, grime and dirt."

I nodded.

We gathered the rest of the yams quickly.

Aka had already prepared the fire pit for cooking. I could see the orange and red flames, and the glow of the coals on the fire.

18

"First, we need to peel the skin of the *katai*," Aka explained. "Then, we can cut the yam up to be cooked."

Aka said we could cook the *katai* three different ways.

First, we needed to cut the yams into small pieces.

"You can cook the yam with coconut milk in a cast iron pot over the fire, or under the ground in *Kupp Mauri* style," Aka explained, as we cut the *katai*. "We'd wrap it in banana leaves to steam the *katai* all day and slow cook it. The last way is to lay them on the coals and roast them... Which one should we do?"

We chose to put the yam pieces
into the iron pot over the fire
Aka had made.

"Aka, can you show me how to cook
the cashew nuts, too?" I asked.

"Yes. While this is cooking, I can
show you how to find and cook
cashew nuts." Aka dusted her
hands off and stood.

"Now, Mira, we need to be careful with this plant," Aka warned. "The sap of the nut and the tree is very dangerous. It can burn your skin and give you blisters. It's always better to have an adult with you when you cook these."

We went over to the cashew tree.

You could cut the fruit off the tree, but you must cook the nut before eating it.

Aka carefully opened a fruit with her knife and picked out the cashew nut.

Then, she dropped it into a bucket of water to wash it off.

We did this with a few of the fruits. After a while, we had enough to roast.

We returned to the fire and removed the *katai*, as they were ready to eat.

I set them aside to cool while Aka put down the bucket of cashew nuts.

"Mira, this is important," Aka said. "I'm going to roast these on the open fire, over the coals. You have to step back for this. The smoke from the cashews is toxic and you shouldn't breathe it in."

I stepped back and walked around the fire, away from the smoke to see them sizzle on the coals.

It didn't take long, and Aka used the tongs to collect the roasted nuts.

We took them and the yams upstairs to the kitchen. We prepared a meal for the rest of the family as they arrived for lunch.

I felt very special, as I had learned a new way of cooking and gathering food for my family to eat.

I couldn't wait to do it again, then teach my children when I'm older.

You can use these questions to talk about this book with your family, friends and teachers.

What did you learn from this book?

Describe this book in one word. Funny? Scary? Colourful? Interesting?

How did this book make you feel when you finished reading it?

What was your favourite part of this book?

About the author

Patricia was born on Thursday Island and is from Meriam-Geauram tribe on her mother's side and Migi Buway-Besi nations on her father's side. She enjoys telling traditional stories to her family. Her favourite story as a child was the 'Monkey and Turtle' story from the islands.

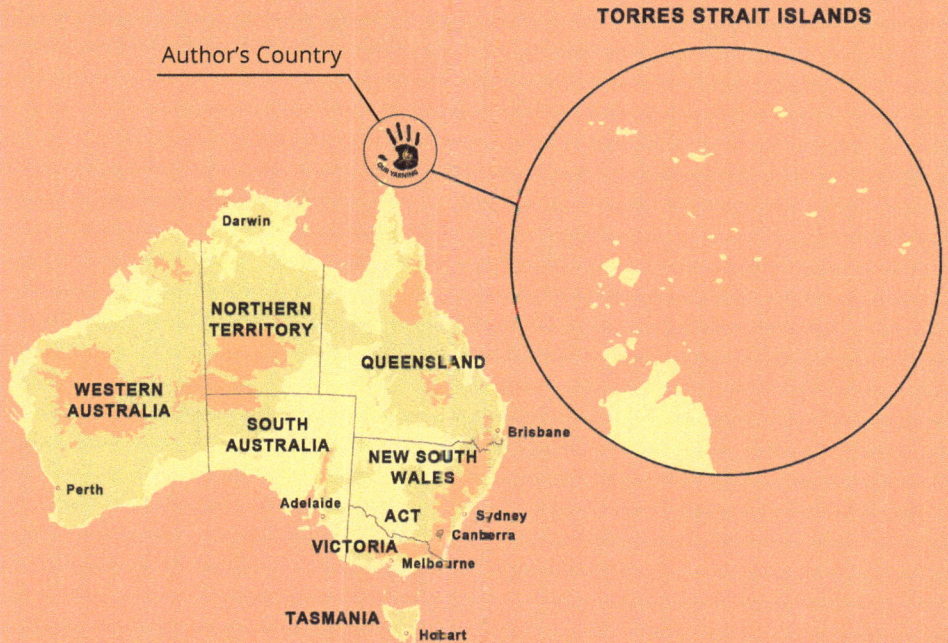

TORRES STRAIT ISLANDS

Author's Country

Darwin

NORTHERN TERRITORY

QUEENSLAND

WESTERN AUSTRALIA

SOUTH AUSTRALIA

Brisbane

Perth

NEW SOUTH WALES

Adelaide

ACT

Sydney

Canberra

VICTORIA

Melbourne

TASMANIA

Hobart

Our Yarning

The Our Yarning collection aligns with the Australian Curriculum through the Cross-Curriculum Priorities — Aboriginal and Torres Strait Islander Histories and Cultures. The collection provides an authentic opportunity for learning and embedding Aboriginal and Torres Strait Islander perspectives because it is written by Aboriginal and Torres Strait Islander people.

We know that children learn better, and enjoy reading more, when they see themselves in the stories, characters and illustrations of the books they read.

To download the app, visit the Google Play Store or Apple Store and search 'Our Yarning'.

libraryforall.org

You're reading Middle Primary

Learner – Beginner readers
Start your reading journey with short words, big ideas and plenty of pictures.

Level 1 – Rising readers
Raise your reading level with more words, simple sentences and exciting images.

Level 2 – Eager readers
Enjoy your reading time with familiar words, but complex sentences.

Level 3 – Progressing readers
Develop your reading skills with creative stories and some challenging vocabulary.

Level 4 – Fluent readers
Step up your reading skills with playful narratives, new words and fun facts.

Middle Primary – Curious readers
Discover your world through science and stories.

Upper Primary – Adventurous readers
Explore your world through science and stories.